Our Cherry Tree Still Stands

As told to Jennifer K. Mittelman

iUniverse, Inc.
New York Bloomington

Copyright © 2009 by Jennifer K. Mittelman

All rights reserved. No part of this book may be used or reproduced by any means, graphic, electronic, or mechanical, including photocopying, recording, taping or by any information storage retrieval system without the written permission of the publisher except in the case of brief quotations embodied in critical articles and reviews.

iUniverse books may be ordered through booksellers or by contacting:

iUniverse
1663 Liberty Drive
Bloomington, IN 47403
www.iuniverse.com
1-800-Authors (1-800-288-4677)

Because of the dynamic nature of the Internet, any Web addresses or links contained in this book may have changed since publication and may no longer be valid. The views expressed in this work are solely those of the author and do not necessarily reflect the views of the publisher, and the publisher hereby disclaims any responsibility for them.

ISBN: 978-1-4401-3607-8 (sc)
ISBN: 978-1-4401-3608-5 (ebook)

Printed in the United States of America

iUniverse rev. date: 05/19/2009

Dedication and Gratitude

For my children, grandchildren, and great-granddaughter, so that generations to come will know our story. I also dedicate this book to my sister Helen.

A special thank you to Tonya for all that you do.

In Memoriam

This book is in memory of the Holocaust victims and the children that were never born. It is a tribute to the memory of my parents, Perle and Joseph, and my little brother, Bela, all of whom perished at Auschwitz. It is also in memory of my brother, Arpie, my sister, Molvin, and my beloved wife, Frida, who was never able to speak about her experience in the concentration camps.

Michael Herskovitz
Bala Cynwyd, PA, 2009

Author's Note

When my grandfather approached me and asked me to help him with a second edition of his book, I was truly honored. My grandpa has always been my hero, and his positive outlook on life has impacted everyone who ever met and came to know him, especially me. I enjoyed our many interviews while doing research with regard to his experiences. I thank my husband, Mike, for his editing expertise, patience, and overall sensitivity for this project, and my family and friends, for their help and support. Special thanks to Shira Cohen for a sensitive and beautifully designed book cover.

In 1992, at age fifteen, I traveled to Poland on a United Synagogue Youth Poland/Israel Pilgrimage and saw five concentration camps, including Auschwitz, the first camp to which my grandfather was taken. I sobbed when I saw the heaps of suitcases, eyeglasses, hair, prosthetic devices, and shoes that now reside in the barracks where prisoners like my grandfather slept. It was an experience that has shaped the person I am today, and one that I will never forget.

In 2008, at age thirty-one, I had the rare opportunity to go back to the village where my grandfather grew up before he was taken away. It was an amazing and life-changing experience.

While we can never fully understand how horrific the Holocaust was, it is our duty as human beings to memorialize the experiences of the survivors. In an age where genocide continues to happen in places like Rwanda and Darfur, it is of paramount importance that we continue to fight against these tragedies and document the stories of the survivors. Please help keep my grandpa's story alive.

Jennifer Mittelman
New York, NY, 2009

Prologue

Imagine growing up in a time and place where your biggest worry was getting home in time for dinner after playing ball with your friends. Imagine not knowing how other people lived elsewhere in the world, never learning about current events, never discussing politics or world events or issues with your parents. Imagine never having heard the word Nazi or the name Adolf Hitler, and then being ripped from your home, never to return. Imagine being taken to a ghetto where you lived in a tent, and then taken to a concentration camp where you would never see your parents or little brother again.

What follows is the story of Miksa (now Michael) Herskovitz, to whom all of those things happened. His memories are those of a very young boy who had no concept of what was happening outside his village. In order to be as accurate as possible, his story has been supplemented with memories furnished by his sister, Helen; stories recorded by his sister, Molvin; and information and photographs from a family trip back to Botfalva, Ukraine, in June 2008. Much of this supplemental information was uncovered between 2006 and 2008. This story is written in his voice.

Chapter One

I was born Miksa Herskovic (pronounced Miksha Hershkovitch) on February 5, 1929, although I also responded to my nickname, Mickey, or, less frequently, Moshe, my Jewish name. My mother, Perle (nee Fried), whose name lives on through both my daughter, Pearl, and niece, Pearl, "wore the pants" in the family. At the time, I was the youngest of four children. Arpie (Jewish name, Naphtali, later called Ernest) was the eldest, born in 1920. My eldest sister was Molvin (Molvina to some, Jewish name, Malkah), born in 1922. Next was Helen (Jewish name, Hana), born in 1925. Our family owned the only grocery store in the village, and my father, Josef—whose name lives on through my nephew, Yossi—ran the store and worked as a milkman as well. My parents were very tolerant, moderate people, who got along with people of all religions and backgrounds. My father was quiet, but very hard working, and unlike me, tall.

We lived in the Trans-Carpathian town of Botfalva, a Czechoslovakian (later turned Hungarian and now Ukrainian) village consisting of fifty or sixty homes, spread along both sides of a dirt road. Most of the villagers were farmers. In fact, the only traffic you faced on our one dirt road was cow traffic! The cows were let out of their respective farms every morning to graze, and at night, they knew how to come home! That was our rush hour. No one in the village had a car. If a car ever drove into the village, everyone came out of their houses to stare at it.

Even 64 years later, the cows were still coming home at the same time!

Botfalva was approximately five kilometers from the city of Ungvar, known today as Uzghorod. The Trans-Carpathian region was known for its cold weather; winters were long and bitter, with so much snow that there were times we could not open our front door because it was too high. Tateh (my father), Arpie, Molvin, and Helen would shovel the snow so we could get out. We were frequently bundled up in heavy winter coats, hats, mittens, and scarves, and donned shoes inside high leather boots that stopped just below our knees.

Our home was one of two Jewish homes in the entire village—the other belonging to my mother's wealthy brother.

Zsiga's house, partially destroyed, but currently inhabited by the woman (and her daughter) who purchased it from Zsiga in the 1950s. At right, the mark of the mezuzah from Zsiga's front door. The current owners say it reminds them forever that a Jewish person once inhabited this home.

We spoke Yiddish amongst ourselves, but when neighbors and friends visited, which happened frequently, we spoke Czech or Hungarian. Our fellow villagers knew we were Jewish but respected our differences. We coexisted extremely well and were often invited to neighbors' homes to share in their customs, such as Easter. While they knew we would not partake in their pig roasts on Christmas, they enjoyed sharing their traditions with us. In exchange, we would routinely give *shalach manos*—packages of food customarily given to friends during the Purim holiday—to our neighbors, and share other Jewish holidays with them as well. Our home was warm and welcoming.

The house where I lived until I was 15 years old.

In fact, our dining room table actually opened up for storage purposes, and on any given day our mother's cakes and breads would fill the inside of the table. My mother would rise at four every Friday morning in preparation for Shabbat, and would bake challah bread, regular bread, and cakes to last us the whole week.

We ate very well—my mother cooked many traditional Eastern European dishes as well as traditional Eastern European Jewish dishes. My favorites were my mother's stuffed cabbage, *cholent* (a heavy stew commonly eaten for lunch on Shabbat and the kosher equivalent of Hungarian goulash) and *kishke* (a dish of kosher beef intestine stuffed with matzo meal, rendered fat, and spices).

We lived on a farm, and actually leased some of our land to fellow villagers who were farmers. Behind our house we had a small stable and an outhouse, and to the side of our house, a well. Our grocery store was attached to the front of our home. There were no cars in our village at that time, but we had a horse and carriage, as well as bicycles. We had no electricity or running water, and we used a wood-burning stove. We also had fruit trees in our yard. To this day,

Helen refuses to eat cherries because she stuffed herself as a child so frequently from our cherry tree that the thought of eating another cherry is unbearable.

Our cherry tree, where Helen spent a lot of time, still standing today.

At left, what used to be the stable in our backyard. At right, our well, still functioning, and what the current owners of the home use as their one-and-only water source. Not pictured: the outhouse, still used.

Compared to others in our village, we were considered financially well off. Most people in Botfalva were only able to eat chicken when one of their chickens became sick and had to be killed. We, on the other hand, ate chicken every Friday night for Shabbat after the *shochet*—the man who performed ritual slaughters in conformity with Jewish law—rode his bicycle to our house to kill the chicken. My parents, religious Jews and just plain good people, frequently gave free food from the store to poor people in our village.

My mother, who the local children called "Pepi Neni" (Mrs. Pepi—short for Perle) was at the store every morning at 7:00 AM (except on Shabbat). Villagers would come in and "forget" their money. She would note it in the books, and tell those villagers to pay "next time," even though she knew they would never be able to pay the money. She also gave cooked food to our poor neighbors. My parents' generosity and warmth commanded great respect from the other villagers and made them well regarded and loved. We knew everyone in our small village and they knew us.

Every morning, my sister Helen would walk to the local farms and supervise the women milking cows. When the women were finished, Helen would carry back heavy containers of milk together with some of the farmers. Some of the containers held between thirty and fifty liters. I have fond memories of going outside our house at night with Arpie, Helen, and Molvin, and with the help of some ropes, lowering the containers down into the well to keep them cool. The following afternoon, we, together with our parents, would transfer the milk into one, two, five, and ten-liter metal containers, which would close hermetically, and be ready for the next morning's delivery.

My father rose at approximately five o'clock every morning to pack up the horse and carriage with the milk containers. He traveled every morning, except the Sabbath, delivering milk to customers in our village and then to the nearby city of Ungvar. The horse knew the route by heart and took my father—and sometimes me if I did not have school—into the city, approximately five kilometers away, where the majority of his customers were. The round-trip route varied between two and three hours. My father would place the appropriate containers in people's doorways and collect the empty ones. To my knowledge, he was paid once per week or month by his customers. While in town, he would also take care of purchasing goods to be sold in our store.

Before going to school every morning—which was located diagonally across the street from our house—but after my father's milk route was completed, I walked with my father and Arpie to synagogue for the *Shacharit,* or morning, prayers. Then, I would return home, cross the street, and go to school.

Today, my old school is used as a church.

A school photograph, taken in front of the school in 1937 (I am second from the top left, in front of the window), which was published in a local newspaper a few years ago. An old neighbor (sixth from the bottom left with the white ribbon in her hair) cut it out and kept it. She showed it to me in June 2008.

I don't have many memories of Arpie because he was nearly ten years older than me, and during most of my childhood, he worked, later serving in the Hungarian army.

Molvin, after completing her high school education, worked as a seamstress in our home. She would sit for hours on end sewing clothing for everyone in our family. In addition, she was frequently commissioned by many villagers to make clothes. My mother, the brains behind our family business, a phenomenal cook, and the one who kept our family organized, was also excellent at sewing. She too sewed dresses for the women in the village. She even made wedding dresses for them!

One of Helen's jobs was to bring Molvin her food and drink, so that Molvin could work continuously. Helen hated doing this and teased Molvin for being bottom heavy, especially since Helen was always riding her bike and was a very thin child and teenager. My mother scolded Helen and warned her not to taunt Molvin because Molvin earned money for our family. Molvin had my mother's personality: she was tough! Once she lifted up a broom at me when she felt I misbehaved and threatened me with, "Wait till Daddy comes home!" The funniest part about that threat was that my father was such a soft-spoken, gentle man. Helen and I take after him in personality, but not in height!

My parents, "Pepi Neni" and Josef Herskovitz

My maternal uncle, Zsiga Fried, had good business sense, like my mother. Zsiga was a very influential and wealthy man in our village and owned multiple horses and tractors for his huge farm and lush fields. Zsiga's machinery was able to make flour and cull seeds from the wheat. In addition to his farming enterprise, Zsiga, owned a cabaret.[1*] Every night after a hard day of labor, the villagers would come to Zsiga's cabaret to drink—it was the only place in the village that served alcohol. Zsiga became very, very wealthy and the unofficial "mayor" of Botfalva.

We were very close to our Uncle Zsiga, as he lived five houses down from us. Helen used to go over there almost daily to help clean because Zsiga's wife was something of a slob, and Helen could not stand seeing dirty dishes in the sink and unmade beds!

Before War World II, neither my parents nor Zsiga ever experienced anti-Semitism. We were all just people, living in the same village, going about our business. While generally life in Botfalva for our family was simple, on reflection it seems our family was more "cosmopolitan" than other families in the village. For example, at one point our family became the only home in the village with a phonograph. We came to have this phonograph because my maternal grandfather, Herman, who had moved to the United States, came to visit us once and brought it. We also had a radio, courtesy of my grandfather. My memory of the first radio was that it was a little box—every afternoon my friends and I would meet in the middle of the street to listen to it for exactly one-half hour. I do not recall ever hearing news reports on the radio. Despite its proximity to Ungvar, our village actually received its news from a man with a drum. He would stop every few houses and beat the drum, wait until people congregated outside, and give a short report. I never saw, much less read, a newspaper, and we never wrote letters to anyone. I do not even believe we had a post office in our village.

---

1 *Note: According to Ellis Island records, Zsiga and Perle's father, Herman Fried, arrived in New York on August 3, 1923, at the age of 64, and listed his profession as cabaret owner.

Up until I was about nine years old, Botfalva was part of Czechoslovakia, after which it was taken over by Hungary. Therefore, my parents spoke Czech and Hungarian to their customers in the store. In school and when my friends and I got together to play ball—mainly football, or soccer as they call it in the United States—we spoke in Czech initially, and later Hungarian. Around the time the Hungarians took over, our few Western luxuries came to an end as well. My grandfather returned from America to die.

He was religious, as were we, and while on his deathbed, he stayed in a room at Zsiga's house. Every morning my grandfather would perform the *Shacharit* prayers in his bed, because he could not get up. One day, Helen was in his room while he was praying. At the conclusion of his prayers, he rested the prayer book on his chest, closed his eyes, and died. He is buried in Botfalva, in an area that is now part of someone else's farm.

The farm area where my maternal grandfather, Herman Fried, is buried.

My parents, siblings and I, together with Uncle Zsiga and his family, were the only Jews in the village of Botfalva. My father's brothers and sisters lived in Komorotz, which was about a two-hour train ride away. We visited them maybe once per year. One of my cousins there, Mendu, had a taxi. It was an old car, but from our small-village perspective, it was a very big deal that he even had a car! Apparently, Mendu made a lot of money from this taxi business. Little did I know that half a century later, I too would dabble in the taxi business.

As I stated previously, we were a religious family. My mother wore a *sheitl* and my father had a short beard, but no *peyas*. I wore a *kippah*. Every Friday night and Saturday our family would walk about two kilometers to and from synagogue in Trusk (pronounced Trushk), a nearly all-Jewish town. On the Sabbath, we would sit in the synagogue for four to five hours. Another large—and probably my least favorite—component of my religious upbringing was my time spent in *heder*. After sitting all day in regular school, with only a one to two hour break in between, I went to religious school for three to four hours every evening in Trusk. *Heder* took place in a room in the synagogue, taught by a rabbi. The rabbi was strict—he had a stick and was not afraid to use it on us. If we did not give the right answer, or talked while he was talking, he would strike us on our backs. All lessons were in Yiddish. We learned about the Jewish holidays, the text of the Torah, and how to chant the Torah. Unlike today's young Jews, we did not learn Hebrew and we did not learn about Israel (then Palestine).

What my parents and uncle were not, however, were scholars, philosophers, or political activists. My parents did not have friends over to discuss politics or Zionism—they had no Jewish friends, and except for Zsiga, no relatives nearby. They were content in their village where they were respected and were able to carry on their traditions comfortably. They were blue-collar business people who got by doing what they needed to do to support their family.

Until a few years ago, I was completely sure that in 1944 my parents had no idea there was a world war going on, or that Jews had been killed by the millions in nearby Poland, Germany, and elsewhere. One thing Helen and I agreed on was that we as kids were extremely naive. We had no idea of what really went on outside our village, with the exception of whatever we saw when we went into town either on the milk route or to buy groceries to stock our store. When World War II began in 1939, I was ten years old, and my baby brother, Bela, had just been born. I had no concept of what a war was. I thought that an airplane flying over us meant war, and we never saw any airplanes in Botfalva. Even though Arpie was serving in the Hungarian army at the time of the German invasion, I thought countries had armies to hold order, as police officers would today. I do not know whether my parents had ever heard of Adolph Hitler. *I* never even knew that name until after World War II.

It took me sixty-two years to find out that Helen, three-and-a-half years older than me, knew differently.

Chapter Two

My worries as a boy were limited to what time I was expected home for dinner, whether I had done my homework, and whether my sisters needed my help in preparing the milk for delivery. My life was simple. My parents shielded me from the world's negativity and knowledge of concentration camps. None of us experienced anti-Semitism. While I will never know what my parents actually knew, I learned from Helen, in 2006, that my parents knew more than they let on. Helen heard our parents discussing the political climate, and when she would ask them what they were talking about, they told her not to ask questions.

To my knowledge, we received our first bits of information about the war from our young man with the drum, followed by German soldiers who made an unwelcome addition to our familiar village scenery.

It was about a month before Passover, 1944, in the morning, when we suddenly saw German soldiers in our village. The drummer came and told us that our village had been taken over. He told us that Jewish children in our village (essentially sisters, my cousins), and me could no longer attend school. They also locked the door to our synagogue. Every Jew was given a yellow star (again, in Botfalva, just our family and Zsiga's) to wear on the outside of our clothes or coat. All of the stars were the same size and it was the village leadership who distributed them to us. My mother sewed the star onto all of our coats. Curiously, Zsiga, by virtue of his status in the community and perhaps because he owned a pub where many German soldiers came to get drunk, was exempt from wearing the yellow star. I can only hypothesize, as I never asked him, that perhaps they used him to get to other Jews in the surrounding areas.

Because I had nothing to do—I could not go to school or *heder*—I hung around the store. I felt a bit different because of the yellow star I now had to wear, but my friends did not say anything or treat me any differently. We Jews also had a curfew, which meant I was not permitted be out after dark. My father eventually abandoned his milk route; he felt too uncomfortable being outside on a frequent basis. Helen, on the other hand, had no fear. She routinely rode her bike into town, even past curfew, to purchase items that we needed for the store or for our family.

A few days or a week later, two German soldiers came into the store. They were tall and young and carried guns at their sides. They walked around the store pretty nicely at first, but then took some merchandise and attempted to leave the store. My father approached them. He must have asked them to pay, which ended up being a big mistake. They soldiers grabbed my father and took him out of the store, to the back. He came back a few minutes later, severely beaten. That was the last time my father ever set foot into the store—the store that my family ran for almost two decades. Just like that, it was all over.

Strangely, even with the yellow stars, curfew, not being able to go to school, a locked synagogue, and my father's beating, I did not feel hated. None of the village people treated me differently or looked at me differently. I simply accepted that the Germans had these rules. I thought my father was beaten because he approached the soldiers in an effort to make them pay—I did not understand at the time that it was because we were Jews. My parents continued to keep me sheltered, even after all of these awful things started happening.

The day after the Germans brutally beat my father, more soldiers came into the store, and they took more and more merchandise. No one stopped them. By then, we could not even replenish our inventory, because having shopped in the city during the milk route—which my father had ceased—our food supply was dwindling. Helen could only carry so many things on her bike, and we needed that food for our family. Finally, after a few weeks, my mother stopped sitting in the store.

Once my parents lost their livelihoods, we were relegated to use whatever resources we had at our disposal. My mother, Helen, and Molvin milked cows to continue providing us some nourishment. We ate sick chickens—my mother was still intent on making sure we had proper Shabbat dinners. When errands were necessary, my mother went out and did them, covering herself as much as possible with a shawl. My father went out as infrequently as possible. Helen, fearless, bought food for us in Ungvar.

After a few weeks of feeling in limbo, my family started feeling stressed and scared. Our neighbors were not mean to us, but they became shy and spoke to us less often. I sensed something bad was going on, but I had no concept of what it was.

According to Helen, my parents must have somehow found out that other Jews in nearby villages had been taken away. Helen saw my mother slicing open the seams of our coats and sewing money in the lining. When Helen asked what she was doing, she told Helen to go away.

Helen also saw our mother write letters to Arpie, who was still in the Hungarian army, telling him that our family was going to a wedding but that she was unsure of when we would return. She wrote in code by using a word that sounded the same but meant two different things in Yiddish and Hungarian, so that if anyone else but Arpie read it, they would not understand the true nature of the note. My mother was instructing Arpie in those letters to visit the Gregus and Balas families in our village, upon his return. My mother took Arpie's clothing to those neighbors' homes, as she must have feared that he would not be able to get back into our home when he returned from the army. Helen questioned my mother as to why she was doing these things, and specifically, why she was taking Arpie's clothing to our neighbor's house. Our mother's response was that Helen should not be asking questions.

Chapter Three

Life as I knew it changed even more drastically early one Shabbat morning just before Passover that year. It was so early that it was still dark outside. My mother woke Molvin, Helen, Bela, and me. She told us to get dressed quickly and to wear layers of clothing, topped off with our coats, which I never knew had money sewn in them. There were soldiers waiting for us by our front door and mama told us we had to leave. We were only half-awake, disoriented and scared. We were raised not to question our parents—as Helen's interaction with my mother demonstrated—and after seeing two soldiers waiting at our front door, we did not voice any questions or utter a single word.

The soldiers told us there was a war and that they were trying to protect us by taking us away to a safe place. The soldiers suggested to my mother that we wear as much clothing as we desired. In addition, we were permitted to bring sixteen kilos of personal effects, roughly 33.6 pounds. We dressed with layers as mama commanded, and we all threw clothes and a few other things into trash bags. We were told we could not take too much.

The soldiers at the door were calm; they did not point or shout at us as movies may depict. To this day, I do not know if those men were Hungarian police, Hungarian soldiers, or German soldiers. They waited until we were dressed and told my father to lock the door to our home and take the key, because he would be the one to reopen it. The soldiers reassured us that they were taking us to safety.

My father never returned to our home.

Chapter Four

Our family (minus Arpie) was taken into a carriage, driven by horses. In my estimation, we were driven 10–15 kilometers to an open area with a white fence around it and a front gate. The carriage pulled us inside the gate. Soldiers ushered us off the carriage and encouraged us to settle into our assigned tent. There were tons of tents, with several families per tent. In addition, there were outhouses. This was our introduction to the ghetto. All we knew was that we would be there for an indeterminate period of time.

In the tent with my parents, sisters, and little brother, I thought about Arpie, and wondered where he was, or if he knew where we were. The Germans prohibited us from leaving the ghetto or receiving visitors. The ghetto was managed by *kapos*, Jews appointed by the Nazis to maintain order amongst us. In the ghetto, the kapos were not mean and we knew they were just like us, forcibly relocated to this ghetto. Every day more and more families arrived.

I am guessing there were 500–1,000 people in the ghetto, all still wearing their stars. I recognized people in the field and knew that these were people from villages and cities close to Botfalva. A makeshift kitchen was created, and we were given dishes and enough food, after standing in line to receive it, so as not to go hungry.

We stayed there for approximately one month, during which time we never stopped thinking we might be going home soon. Having nothing else to do, we boys got together every day and played. My siblings and I never asked our parents questions about anything related to our situation or the war, and they never discussed those topics with us either. I do not know if our parents did not want to scare us, or whether they just did not know how to talk to us about such adult things. I can only imagine that other parents were similarly uncommunicative with their children, as I received no information from the boys with whom I played on a daily basis. We were kept in the dark and were afraid to ask questions.

One afternoon, I left my tent to pick up a new friend from his tent, so we could play. When I arrived at the tent, it was empty. I noticed a few other empty tents. Families were leaving the ghetto without any explanation on a daily basis. Before I could wrap my head around what was actually going on in the ghetto and where my fellow Jews were being taken after they left the ghetto, soldiers came to our family's tent. I do not know if they were Hungarian or German soldiers, but they told us to take our things and that we had to leave. Things were still calm—there were no guns pointed at us and the soldiers displayed no violence. We simply followed directions and got onto a horse-and-buggy along with some other families. I somehow found out that because we were Jewish they were moving us to a camp with better facilities, where we would be permitted to work.

Chapter Five

We were taken to the only railroad station in Ungvar, where we saw cattle cars on the train tracks and an endless sea of faces surrounding us, while we waited for our next directive. The sideline of the train track was busy—we did all we could to try and stay close to each other.

My family and I waited about an hour-and-a-half before being loaded into one of the cattle cars. There were cattle cars as far back as I could see on the track. Each car contained people just like us, families trying to stay together. We were scared, but at that point, we did not fear for our lives—we were under the impression we were going to be transferred to a place where we would work.

The car was crowded, although there was enough space for everyone to sit down. We had no idea where we were going, but we spent two nights and a full day on that cattle car. I did not sleep the entire way. The soldiers' version of kindness was to give us cans of food to share with each other, like animals. The restroom in the cattle car consisted of a bucket placed in one corner of the cattle car, covered up with a blanket. The smell was awful. Every time the train stopped to pick up more people, someone emptied the bucket.

Soldiers guarded every car at each stop along the way. Usually there was just one soldier per car, standing at the door. They did leave the doors slightly open, along with two windows for air. Each stop meant different soldiers not seen before. Later, I heard that most of the soldiers at the earlier stops did not actually know where the trains were going either.

Throughout the journey, people talked, but I was scared, and everyone around me seemed scared. No one tried to escape the train.

No one had the guts to try because, while it went unspoken, we all knew we would be shot if we tried.

Although I did not have much of a concept of how many times we stopped, I am pretty sure we stopped at every major city en route to Auschwitz, in Poland. At every train station, more cattle cars filled with people would be connected to the end of train, but no one entered our cattle car. As we got closer to what would be our destination, the soldiers demanded our valuables. The soldiers spoke in German, which we did not understand, but someone in the car translated it into Yiddish. The soldiers also asked for our money. The soldiers became more belligerent the closer we got to the camp. At the last stop, before arriving at Auschwitz, they took our trash bags, with all of our belongings, and dumped the contents on top of our heads. I watched the soldiers collect people's money and watches. I knew that if people did not hand over their valuables, they would get punished. I did not realize, however, that some people who handed over their valuables would die just hours later anyway.

Chapter Six

Auschwitz

Mayhem. The beginning of the worst possible thing that could ever happen to a human being. The last stop on the train, Auschwitz, would be my parents' and Bela's last stop on earth.

The gate to Auschwitz

It was a gray day. The soldiers put ramps on the cars—cattle chutes. Hundreds of armed German soldiers stood waiting together with their German shepherd dogs. The sounds came from everywhere all at once: people in hysterics and screaming; babies, children, and adults crying; gunshots pounding; and vicious dogs barking. Soldiers pushed us down and out of the car and everyone just tried to stay together. Staying together was the only objective at that moment, apart from staying alive. We screamed for each other and cried because we were so scared and nervous. Thousands of others similarly situated only amplified the horrendous sounds of that morning. The soldiers fired their guns to scare people and quiet them down. German shepherds barked loudly and viciously with the intent to provoke fear.

The Germans pushed the crowd through a gate, above which stated, "*Arbeit Macht Frei*"—"Work makes you free." I could translate it because it was so similar to Yiddish.

Immediately after passing through this gate, separation and selection began.

"Men to the right! Women to the left!" screamed the Nazi camp guards.

We had worked so hard and for so long to stay together, just like every other family, that any separation between us was too difficult to bear. The separation was instantaneous—families were torn apart, in many cases, forever. The Nazis used brutal force, having no qualms about beating parents just to divide them from their children. The Nazis threw children into closed trucks and drove away with them. My mother would not let go of Bela. Before I realized what was happening, I witnessed the Nazis throwing my mother and Bela into the closed trucks with the rest of the children and mothers who would not let go.

I never got to say goodbye. It was the last time I ever saw my mother or my baby brother.

As per the soldiers' orders, my father and I walked to the right. Helen and Molvin went to the left.

Further division then began. On the men's side, older men went in one direction, teenagers and young men in the other. My father and I went in the same direction. Had I been a bit smaller, skinnier, or younger, my fate would have been far different. I clung to my father. We knew immediately we were all we had.

The Nazis ordered us to stand in line and create five rows. They forced us to undress and told us we were going to take a shower and to remember where we left our clothes. We all arranged our clothes in different ways so as to find them easily after the shower: some placed their shoes atop their clothing; others placed their hat atop their pile. After undressing, the Nazis ushered us into a big building that looked like a warehouse. Helen told me later that the women had a similar experience, only it was all the more humiliating for them to be naked.

Barbers lined the walls on two sides of the warehouse we entered. Hundreds of us went in, one behind the next. As we walked past the barbers, they removed our hair from head to toe (including underarms). The barbers were Jews, spared by the Nazis for their ability to perform free labor for the Germans. Water covered the bottom of the warehouse floor, reaching the middle of my calf—about one foot high. Though we had been told we were entering the warehouse to take showers, there were no showers inside. This was one of many mind games played by the Nazis.

After walking through the warehouse naked—with wet feet and no hair—we saw picnic tables that were manned by either kapos or soldiers. I still had my father with me. On each table, there were shirts, pants, and shoes. We were ordered to take one of each—obviously, we were not getting our clothing back. Again, this was a mind game. Hundreds or thousands of men with no hair, no personal belongings, and the same prisoner uniforms meant no individuality. We were stripped not only of body hair and family, but also of our dignity as people. We did not receive identification-number tattoos, as did many of the earlier prisoners. While I will never know exactly why, some theorize it is because it was so late in the war.

We exited into a courtyard supervised by *kapos*. As I said previously, *kapos* were Jews like us, but handpicked by the Nazis to do some of their dirty work and make sure we obeyed orders. In the camps, the *kapos* were crueler than in the ghetto. Some prisoners, like Helen, swear that many of the *kapos* treated them worse than the German soldiers did. Generally speaking, the *kapos* were Polish Jews who had been at the camps for years prior to our arrival. One actually told Helen that she had no sympathy for her because, while Helen had been playing at home, she had been suffering at the camp. Weeks after my arrival, however, I befriended a few *kapos,* who told me about the gas chamber and crematorium. They were the ones who told me and my fellow prisoners what went on in the rest of the camp. However, it was during my first interaction with the *kapos* in that courtyard, on my first day in Auschwitz, that I knew I was a prisoner. My clothing had black stripes, just like someone in jail.

We were told we could exchange our clothing with other prisoners to find shirts, pants, and clothes that fit us better. Although there was a lot of confusion, I somehow found people with whom to exchange my shirt, pants, and shoes. Once I had dressed with a more properly fitting uniform, I realized I could not find my father.

I never saw him again.

* * * * *

The *kapos* and soldiers grabbed teenagers of similar size to me and gathered us together. They separated sets of twins from the main group. A pair of twins from Trusk who were on my transport were separated from me around this time. I never saw them again either.

Those of us remaining, with the exception of twins, marched out from the courtyard and into the *lager,* or camp. At this point, I noticed for the first time the orchestral music that played twenty-four hours a day. Driveways separated the *lagers* to make room for jeeps. Soldiers stood ground in watchtowers around all the *lagers*. People were grouped according to certain classifications. The gypsies went into the *gypsylager,* the children went into the *kinderlager,* and soon, we were separated from the grownups.

Each *lager* consisted of thirty-two barracks. Nazi soldiers ushered us to our barracks, which contained thirty-two sets of three-level bunk beds. The *kapos* screamed for us to get onto the wooden bunk beds, where six of us shared a wood frame and bed, sans mattress. When the barracks filled up, the guards closed the doors, and we waited. Quietly.

We must have gotten into our barracks by 1:00 or 2:00 PM. Approximately four hours later, the soldiers blew a whistle and called us out to do *appel,* or lineup. I found out we were in *Lager A*, across from the women's *lager*. Some people in *Lager A* were screaming; they actually saw women they knew. I never saw Helen or Molvin, but they remember seeing me, and, once, my father. Helen told me a story of which I have no memory. According to Helen, I saw her through a fence, and told her that I had managed to get some cherries for her. I tied the cherries into a sack of some kind and threw them over the fence for her.

Every morning when we heard the whistle, we ran out for *appel*. We had to be dressed with pants and shoes, but no shirt. Group by group we ran to the building to get washed. The soldiers ran next to us. We had only a few minutes—almost no time at all—and we were constantly under armed escort. After washing, we stood back in line for breakfast, which consisted of a tiny bit of soup and bread with either a piece of cheese or butter.

After our morning "meal," we stood at attention until the soldiers inspected us, always removing those of us who appeared weak, tired, sick, or had a look on their face that the soldier did not like. Being pointed at meant you were removed—gone—permanently. The soldiers looked us dead in the eye. Three times a week, the infamous Dr. Mengele—a German physician who performed monstrous medical experiments on many inmates and almost all the twins—inspected us.

The lineups also afforded the soldiers the opportunity to choose a handful of us to work. The rest of us remained standing until we were sent back to our barracks. The barracks had concrete floors, which we younger teenagers had the task of washing and squeegeeing daily.

Several times, the Nazis made me pick potatoes from nearby fields or go to a cinderblock factory to do heavy lifting. One time, after packing bricks at a nearby factory, the guards forced me to carry the bricks with a wooden contraption on my back to a separate place for piling.

The guards took the adult males to work every morning—they went on a truck through the *Lager A* gate, went to work, and came back at night. When they did not have enough labor, they started taking some of us. When we were taken out of the camp to perform labor, we were always accompanied by armed soldiers and German shepherd dogs. We joined the men on the trucks. Every time we left the camp, we saw the ironic and iconic gate, *Arbeit Macht Frei*. The soldiers forced us to count ourselves in the truck when leaving the camp. The rule was that the same amount of prisoners had to return. Dead or alive.

Sometimes prisoners died during our labor excursions. Perhaps they did not do their job to the soldiers' satisfaction. Perhaps they collapsed. Many dead bodies returned in the truck having been shot, beaten, or otherwise murdered.

I will never forget many of the cruel and inhuman things those soldiers did to us. The most sadistic thing I witnessed occurred during one of the times I was chosen to leave the camp and perform physical labor. The guards drove me and several other prisoners to a farm on a hill. Countless rocks lay everywhere at the bottom of the hill. The guards provided us with wheelbarrows and shovels and told us to push the rocks up the hill in the wheelbarrows. The guards instructed other prisoners to remain at the top of the hill and load the rocks onto the truck. I worked next to two German soldiers at the bottom of the hill.

Out of nowhere, I heard one of the soldiers say to the other, "Look at the Jew that's not moving his wheelbarrow [or moving it too slow]. You could aim and shoot him right between the eyes." And so the other one did. He aimed and shot the prisoner dead.

The day ended and we loaded up on the truck to head back to our *lager*. There were a few dead people, including the unfortunate man whom the Nazis thought was not moving his wheelbarrow fast enough and another man beaten to death. We placed our dead comrades back on the truck according to the Nazi rule—return to the *lager* with as many bodies as left the *lager*, dead or alive.

After evening *appel*, the Germans gave us soup and bread for dinner. They allowed us to walk around a bit after eating and it was during these walks that we could see into the girls' *lager*. Approximately twice a week at 5:00 or 6:00 PM, we heard sirens blaring throughout the camp. Upon hearing the ear-piercing noise, everyone hurriedly rushed back to his own barracks.

A perimeter of barbed wire, charged with 440 volts of electricity, surrounded the *lagers*. Two men from my *lager* tried to grab the wires. They died instantly. Most of us, however, did not create plans to escape. For one, there was nowhere to go. More important, we knew that any attempt to escape would result in sirens blaring, dogs barking, and soldiers ready to fire. We needed to be in our barracks, or risk facing terrible consequences.

Every day I hoped to see my father; I was so shaken up the first few days in Auschwitz. I knew Bela had my mother, and Molvin and Helen had each other. I wanted my father. As the days turned into months, I still held out hope that I would run into him. I repeatedly inspected all the prisoners to try and find him. Other than that, I looked at the sky a lot. I did not think about God; I did not pray; I did not think about anything specific. I repeatedly told myself, "One more day, one more day, one day at a time." Every day I hoped that, somehow, I would see my father again. I knew I had to survive, so I could see my entire family again and tell them what happened to me.

After a while, I stopped thinking about going home. My thought was just to get through the day without being beaten or killed. Considering the fate of most of the other prisoners, I know that I was lucky to have survived with only one beating. I still have the scar from when a soldier cut my right hand with a sharp knife after he caught me trying to steal some bread. For whatever the reason, I did not fear being taken to the gas chamber. Rather, because I had entered Auschwitz at an average weight, I feared that I would collapse from hunger and die. Deep down, I hoped I would survive. I knew I would have a lot to tell my mama and papa when I got back home, and I never stopped thinking and hoping that, someday, I would return with my family to Botfalva.

Gradually the number of teenagers my age dwindled. Each night, between six and nine o'clock, sirens wailed to alert us to be on our block. Once or twice a week, one whole block was evacuated. We figured those prisoners were taken to the gas chamber where the Jewish workers appeared strong and healthy.

One night, for a reason I cannot now articulate, we had a feeling that our block was next to be taken. About thirty of us escaped from our barracks through a window in the bathroom, even though it had barbed wire. We did not care that we were getting cut up severely—we just knew we needed to get out. We helped each other out the window and tried to make an escape to another block. It was nighttime, and the sirens blared once someone got wind of our escape. I found myself in front of the twins' block. A guard grabbed me and asked me if I belonged in that barracks. I said yes. He threw me inside. I slid under a bunk bed and lay there for a few days. One morning after *appel*, I walked out of the twins' barracks and back to my own block. I saw a lot of new faces. I don't know how many of my fellow escapees actually survived that night.

That was Auschwitz. It claimed more than half a year of my life.

Chapter Seven

Mauthausen

```
KL.:                                              Häftl.-Nr.:
                                                  134309 Ung. Jude
              Häftlings-Personal-Karte
Fam.-Name: Herskovits        Überstellt      Personen-Beschreibung:
Vorname:   Miklos           am:      an KL.  Grösse:           cm
Geb. am:   20.10.29 Botfalva                 Gestalt:
Stand:     led.    Kinder:                   Gesicht:
Wohnort:   Botfalva Com. Ungvar              Augen:
Strasse:   Fö Str. 61       am:      an KL.  Nase:
Religion:  mos. Staatsang.: Ung.             Mund:
Wohnort d. Angehörigen: Vater  am:   an KL.  Ohren:
           Jozsef w.o.                       Zähne:
                            am:      an KL.  Haare:
Eingewiesen am: 27.4.44 Au                   Sprache:
durch:                      am:      an KL.
in KL.: 28.11.44 Ba. 26.2.45 KLM             Bes. Kennzeichen:
Grund: Ung. Jude           Entlassung:
Vorstrafen:                 am:   durch KL.: Charakt.-Eigenschaften:
                           mit Verfügung v.: Sicherheit b. Einsatz:
              Strafen im Lager:
      Grund:        Art:        Bemerkung:
                                             Körperliche Verfassung:
```

According to a registration card from Mauthausen, I arrived in Mauthausen on November 28, 1944, and left Mauthausen on February 26, 1945. It also says I arrived at Auschwitz on April 27, 1944. It describes me as a Hungarian Jew. My birth date is wrong on the card, though the year is correct, and it lists my name as Miklos instead of Miksa.

One day, without warning, the Germans forced me and many other prisoners to march to another camp: Mauthausen. We walked day and night, passing through many fields and lots of rotten potatoes. Along the way, fellow prisoners who couldn't walk further were coaxed by the soldiers to just sit down. Once seated, a truck drove by and picked them up. Just like that, their fate was sealed.

Mauthausen was in Austria. I later learned we were evacuated from Auschwitz because the Russian forces were advancing and the

Nazis were trying to hide us. Mauthausen was classified as a Category 3 camp, the fiercest designation before death camp. Prisoners were to be exterminated by death or had the designation of "return not desired." When I arrived to Mauthausen, there was less division than at Auschwitz. Older children and teenagers, like me, were mixed in to barracks with adults. The Germans no longer used us for labor; instead, we mainly laid around and lined up. Every day the guards removed a few people from our lineups. There were no gas chambers or crematoria at Mauthausen.

Mauthausen was a much smaller camp. Whereas Auschwitz was made up of many *lagers*, Mauthausen had only one. There were far fewer prisoners there, as well—many people did not survive the walk from Auschwitz. At that point, I had no spirit and I did not care or think about anyone or anything. We lived like animals—there were no washing facilities, and we were only permitted to go to the bathroom at certain times. I still wore the same prisoner uniform I had received at Auschwitz. People collapsed daily; it became routine. We were no longer shocked to see a person drop dead.

Because we were little more than walking corpses, there was no work schedule, and we did nothing all day or night. We were fed barely enough to stay alive. A carriage with horses brought food in daily. The soldiers did not even need guns or dogs anymore; we were too weak to resist or threaten them in any way. We could barely walk; it was obvious the soldiers had no fear that we would run.

I was in Mauthausen for a few months before the Germans transferred me to my third and final concentration camp: Gunskirchen.

Chapter Eight

Gunskirchen and Liberation

Of all the horrors of the place, the smell, perhaps, was the most startling of all. It was a smell made up of all kinds of odors—human excreta, foul bodily odors, smoldering trash fires, German tobacco—which is a stink in itself—all mixed together in a heavy dank atmosphere, in a thick, muddy woods, where little breeze could go. The ground was pulpy throughout the camp, churned to a consistency of warm putty by the milling of thousands of feet, mud mixed with feces and urine. The smell of Gunskirchen nauseated many of the Americans who went there. It was a smell I'll never forget, completely different from anything I've ever encountered. It could almost be seen, and hung over the camp like a fog of death.

Captain J.D. Pletcher, Berwyn, Illinois, of the 71st Infantry, the American liberators of Gunskirchen

As we entered the camp, the living skeletons still able to walk crowded around us and, though we wanted to drive farther into the place, the milling, pressing crowd wouldn't let us. It is not an exaggeration to say that almost every inmate was insane with hunger. Just the sight of an American brought cheers, groans, and shrieks. People crowded around to touch an American, to touch the jeep, to kiss our arms—perhaps just to make sure that it was true. The people who couldn't walk crawled out toward our jeep. Those who couldn't even crawl propped themselves up on an elbow, and somehow, through all their pain and suffering, revealed through their eyes the gratitude, the joy they felt at [our] arrival ....

Captain J.D. Pletcher.

Gunskirchen was a sub-camp of Mauthausen. I cannot remember how long it took to walk there from Mauthausen; all I can recall is that one day the Germans simply lined us up and told us to walk. Gunskirchen was essentially an area of forest surrounded with white, barbed-wire fences, German guards, and guns. At the gate to the camp, there were about ten fifty-five-gallon drums, filled with a liquid we thought to be water, which we were forbidden to touch. It was spring, which meant it was rainy but not yet warm. Gunskirchen had neither barracks nor tents. Instead, we slept on the muddy ground outside. Guards fed us just once a day, instead of twice, as we had become accustomed to at the other camps.

At Gunskirchen, I saw a Jew in civilian clothes for the first time. The Nazis brought the Jewish soldiers they had captured from all over Europe. Some of them may have been American Jewish soldiers or perhaps other resistance fighters. Just as the Nazis did to us in the cattle cars, they stole anything of value from these Jewish soldiers. Every day, more and more Europeans arrived at Gunskirchen. We were all together—there was no separation. Some of us looked like skeletons, while the recently arrived Europeans looked radically different.

If Mauthausen was bad, Gunskirchen was that much worse. Gunskirchen was very well hidden in the "Hochholz," a young pine forest that was so dense it did not let much sunshine through. We were completely covered in lice, head to toe. There were no toilets, just holes in the ground. Those who were not strong enough to walk the entire way to the designated toileting hole were shot. Dead bodies were strewn about. When it rained, we were literally stuck outside in the mud, walking between trees. I spent most of my days sitting next to a tree and falling asleep.

There was a clearing in the camp where some cows pulled a flatbed carriage. It came once a day with thirty-gallon trash containers full of "soup"—our one meal per day, in the middle of the day. The carriage pulled in and the containers were dumped onto the ground. Every day, we would pick up a container from the mud and stand in line for this soup. We ate while walking in a circle, and once finished, we dropped the containers on the ground. We were so desperate for food that one time, when someone threw some type of explosive near the cows and carriage, killing the cows and a few prisoners, we all ran to pick up the pieces of raw meat that exploded nearby. To this day, I have no idea what type of meat I ate. All I knew was it was meat, and I was starving.

We awoke every morning to new corpses, which were removed later in the day. As soon as we spotted a corpse, we stole its clothes and left its body there to be picked up later. We had been turned into savage animals.

For the most part, days ran into nights. On and on, it continued. Until liberation. That morning, I woke up to the sound of multiple gunshots. At some point in the afternoon, I noticed the gates were open. I did not see any German soldiers, yet their uniforms were strewn upon the ground. I saw other people awakening and noticing the absence of soldiers, ever-present since our deportation. Gradually, we started walking towards the gate. First though, we opened the large drums at the gate, hoping to drink water. Rather than water, the drums were filled with gasoline. The soldiers had those drums there so that in an emergency, they could torch the entire camp.

Exactly three months after my sixteenth birthday, on May 5, 1945, about five of us, all around my age, walked out of the camp. The field suddenly turned green after the muddy brown we knew so well. We walked to where we could see what appeared to be a main street, not too far from where the camp had been. As we walked into the small valley preceding the main street, we saw military tanks and trucks. We did not know the intentions of this new military force, so we laid our bodies down in the sand in hopes of hiding or finding mercy. The tank stopped and opened. One soldier exited the tank and had five-pound cans of hamburger meat. He threw the cans over the side of the tank to us. We grabbed fistfuls of meat with our sandy hands and started shoving it in our mouths.

The next thing I knew, I was in a hospital in Munich.

Chapter Nine

Helen and Molvin

The only firsthand female perspectives I have about camp life are from Helen and, to some extent, a written recollection from Molvin.

I asked Helen if she too had to run to the showers half-undressed. She told me that, no, they were fully dressed when they ran to the showers, but they had female *kapos* accompanying them. They left their clothes in a huge pile upon entering the showers at Auschwitz, and then they grabbed anyone's clothes afterwards.

Helen stayed together with Molvin almost the entire time they were in camps. Other prisoners who had been in the camps for a period of time before Helen and Molvin's arrival advised them not to let anyone know they were sisters, for fear the Nazis would separate them or kill one of them to keep the other in line.

During her four months of hell in Auschwitz, Helen explained that like the men, every day they stood in line for inspection by Dr. Mengele. Mengele looked for girls under the age of eighteen, and he required that the girls stand before him naked. Each day, he selected five girls to take to an unknown location. One day, Mengele included Helen in this selection of five, and she separated from Molvin for the first time. One of the evil *kapos* told Helen and the other chosen girls that, as a result of their selection, they were going to have a wonderful life and even wear white gloves. Once left alone with another, more humane *kapo*, however, Helen and the other selected teenage girls learned they were going to be used as whores for the Nazis. They would indeed have everything they wanted, but as soon as the Nazi soldier was tired of his girl, she would be killed. The *kapo* told the five girls that she would leave the door to their barracks open that night, so that they could escape and run back to their original barracks. The *kapo* advised the girls to stay low so as to avoid the ever-flashing lights from the Nazi watchtowers. After dark, the five girls tried to escape. The sirens sounded, and three of the five young women were shot and killed. Helen and one other girl managed to survive and make their way back to their original barracks, where she reunited with Molvin.

There is no doubt that not having a tattoo saved Helen. The next day at *appel,* she made sure to get to the front of the line. When the soldiers counted the girls and there were more at the *appel* than there should have been, the last few women to be counted were killed.

After four months, Helen and Molvin were transferred to Torun, a sub-camp of Stutthof. My sisters traveled by covered wagon to Buchenwald where they stayed overnight, then were taken back again before sunrise the next morning. They traveled for many more days in the wagon until they arrived at Torun. Women were not permitted to wear normal clothes, as in Auschwitz, but instead received gray prison nightgowns, almost like a potato sack, with an identifying number sewed onto it. They were not given shoes, but they did take part of the bottom of their long dresses and covered their heads with them, to obscure the fact that they had been shaved.

Helen and Molvin, young women at this time, performed daily manual labor at the Nazis' command. Helen dug ditches day after day. The ditches became deeper than the women were tall, and often the weakening women had difficulty pulling themselves out of the ditch at the conclusion of the workday. An older Nazi, who had been relatively kind to Helen, advised her to jump and make noise with the shovel while in the ditch so the other soldiers would think she was working. Nevertheless, the Nazis beat Helen on the back frequently with heavy iron shovels when they saw her take a break. She was beaten so badly that her back broke multiple times. Helen knew that complaining would mean death, so she suffered quietly, and her broken back healed crooked.

One time, Helen's fingers and toes froze and blistered, and the guards took her to a "hospital" barrack. She suffered from a fever. The same older Nazi who helped Helen in the ditches came into the hospital and encouraged her to leave the hospital barracks and return to work. Most prisoners sent to the hospital barracks were executed soon thereafter.

Towards the end of the war, the Germans forced Helen, Molvin, and many other women to line up and walk out of the camp. They walked for days, maybe a week, trudging through a heavy snow and sleeping in farms along the way. Animals kicked them and relieved themselves on the women. Women who could not walk anymore were shot. They received no food for the entire week and survived by eating snow. At the end of the journey, they arrived to the actual city of Torun where they were locked in a prison. They heard shooting and bombs outside.

Helen, Molvin, and the other women were warned against escaping out the windows. Of course, they looked out the windows, and saw German soldiers running. Buildings had been bombed with explosives and Russian soldiers ran in.

The Russians opened the doors to the prison and started screaming, "Everybody out!" Helen and Molvin knew they were free, and they were excited, but they did not know where to go. The Russians led them to bakeries and other vacant homes and encouraged them to eat. Helen saw many people die, after surviving the hell of the concentration camps, from eating too much. The Russians then ushered all of the remaining prisoners onto a train. Neither Helen nor Molvin had any idea where they were going. All of a sudden, after traveling for some time, the train stopped. The train tracks had been bombed and they could not continue. They ended up taking the train back to where they started. The city was completely bombed and looting commenced. They looted bakeries and vacant homes to find food to eat—even the mayor of the town helped them. Helen also found a coat with a fur collar, which she wore to stay warm. The fur collar was full of lice.

After a day or two of Helen, Molvin, and the other prisoners sleeping on the ground with the animals, the Russian soldiers completed repairs to the tracks and everyone reboarded the train. They rode that train all the way to Ungvar, known today as Uzghorod. Zsiga knew that prisoners were returning daily, and so he, along with two friends, waited by the train every day hoping to find his wife and children, his sister, brother-in-law, and his nieces and nephews. That was how he found Helen and Molvin.

Helen gets choked up when she recalls Uncle Zsiga telling a rabbi that she had come home to die, but that at least he could make a proper funeral for her. Helen weighed sixty-five pounds when she came home from the war and could not hold down food. She endured a four-year hospital rehabilitation in Europe, several dangerous back surgeries, and further rehabilitation in the United States, including having to relearn how to walk.

Chapter Ten

When I regained consciousness in the Munich hospital, I learned that I had typhus. I weighed forty-five kilos (roughly ninety-six pounds). I had no idea what happened to the other boys who shared the meat with me.

I stayed in the hospital until I was able to walk, eat normally, and perform basic daily functions. I learned later that a lot of prisoners who managed to survive similar conditions died of typhus. I felt lucky to have survived, yet again.

Once my medical providers were satisfied with my progress, the doctors sent me to Budapest for rehabilitation where I stayed for several months. In Budapest, I met some Red Cross workers (or the equivalent) who searched for my family. They found my Uncle Zsiga, who was back in Botfalva. They contacted him and he came to Budapest to get me. He took me back to our village where my sisters had also made their way. Arpie had also returned home. Sadly, neither our parents nor Bela ever came back.

Upon arriving back "home," we realized that the Ukrainians had taken over our village—and more specifically, our home. Impossible to believe, but they treated us almost worse than the Germans. They did not want to recognize us as citizens because we were Jewish. Time and war had changed our village from the peaceful home we knew growing up.

While with Zsiga, we slept in a barn. Zsiga's house, as well as ours, had been taken away. Zsiga's home was housing Ukrainian soldiers.

After the war, I stopped keeping kosher and refrained from going to synagogue. I was angry and opposed to religious observance of

Judaism. The image of my father being pulled by his beard affected me more profoundly than I knew and, subconsciously, turned me off to anything reminding me of my religion as practiced before the war. I also felt that strict observance of Judaism disadvantaged me and the lifestyle I wanted. I hated the thought of being limited in terms of what I could eat or when I could travel. To me, being a non-religious Jew equaled freedom.

Freedom as a Jew, however, was not something we could find in the Ukrainian version of our old village. Due to vehement anti-Semitism in the region, all the Jews who had returned there after the war tried to leave. We all wanted to go to Czechoslovakia, which was not anti-Semitic. There were plenty of Jews living in Carlsbad (now called Karlovy Vary). Nevertheless, we would have to escape at a place on the border, designated only by wires.

One dark night, we all snuck our way into Czechoslovakia through a spot Arpie had found in advance where fewer soldiers stood guard. I wriggled on my belly under the fence. Arpie had actually tried to cross the border a few days after I returned from the camps, but he was arrested and taken to jail. Zsiga bailed him out, at which point Arpie went back to Ungvar and met up with some friends his age. He got connected with some non-Jews and, somehow, someone that he knew sent him papers so that he could emigrate to Canada. Unfortunately, because of our age difference and the fact that we had spent more time apart than together, I did not really know him or why he chose Canada.

Helen, Molvin, and I stayed in Czechoslovakia for about three years with Zsiga, who had lost his wife and children in the camps.

At that point, it was 1948. Within three years after our small family reunion, Helen and Molvin married. Helen married Willie Goodman, someone whose family we knew before the war. Molvin married Itzik Schvartz. I began training to become an auto mechanic, having started working in a garage fixing tractors and other farm equipment. One day I saw an advertisement inviting any Jew over a certain age who was willing to fight for the brand new State of Israel to volunteer for training. Without a second thought, I decided that was what I wanted to do. It ended up being one of the best decisions I ever made in my life.

Chapter Eleven

During the time I trained in Czechoslovakia to be a soldier for Israel, I met the woman who would later become my wife. I was living with Helen, her husband Willie, and my little niece, Pearl, in Carlsbad at the time.

Frida and I met briefly during our training time in Czechoslovakia. She too survived the concentration camps, and to me she was beautiful. Like me, all her siblings, except her little brother, survived the camps; and she also lost her parents. I never learned much more about Frida's experience in the camps; she could not bring herself to talk about it.

Two weeks after the conclusion of our training in Czechoslovakia, many of us journeyed on a train to Italy, the first leg of our journey to Israel. I saw Frida again then, and we chatted. I found out that one of her sisters, Goldie (Zahava), and her only brother, Mordechai, were also moving to Israel. Frida planned to live with them.

Once we reached Italy, we transferred to the bottom of a freight ship to make passage to Israel. We arrived in Israel at the end of 1948 and were immediately brought to an army training camp. There we received Israeli *Tzahal* (Israeli Defense Forces) uniforms and guns. The women also received uniforms, but no guns. Frida worked an office job. We learned Hebrew quickly, because we had no choice.

Because we worked really hard all day, the army provided us with dance parties every night to relax and let out some steam. Of course some of us needed to remain on duty during the dance parties too, so we couldn't relax every night. One night I saw Frida while on duty and gave her a kiss. She ran away.

I would not be deterred though. Her blue eyes were worth it to try again! A few days later, I saw her at one of the dances and asked her to dance. We dated and danced from that point forward. It was not completely smooth, however. I had to pass her brother Mordechai's inspection before I was permitted to marry her. I used to travel two hours one-way just to see her.

I served in the Israeli army from 1948–1951. In fact, I was still a soldier when Frida and I married. The army offered me a contract to stay in the army—they were prepared to give us a home! However, Frida told me if I stayed in the army, she would not marry me. Obviously, she meant more to me than anything, so I did not sign up again. We married on September 23, 1951, in a big auditorium in northern Israel's Har HaCarmel—Mount Carmel. Frida was a few weeks shy of her twenty-third birthday, and I was twenty-two years old.

After we married, we lived in Bat Galim (also in the north of Israel) near an old friend of Frida's parents, "Uncle" Moshe Binyamini. Uncle Moshe must have been in Israel for quite some time because, by 1951, he already had a job at a port in the north and a nice apartment.

I had been living up there before we married, serving as a transportation sergeant. The government provided me with a tiny, tin shack. The shack had an outdoor shower with no water—I had to use a bucket to wash myself. I shared this shack with my friend Meyer Berkovitch, whom I had reconnected with in Haifa. He was Arpie's age, and from the village next to Botfalva.

My job in the army, as transportation sergeant, was to send trucks to places they were needed, and I drove around in a jeep making sure things ran smoothly. When Frida and I married, my roommate left our shack and my new wife moved in. She immediately took work on a nearby farm, picking vegetables.

Uncle Moshe loaned us some money to purchase an old truck. After my release from the army, I subcontracted privately for the military and became my own boss at a young age. With my old truck, I delivered military supplies from one army camp to another. *Tzahal* paid me, while Frida waitressed at an Arab-owned restaurant in Haifa, near the port.

Chapter Twelve

Frida and I both worked night and day to make ends meet while we lived in the tiny shack. After a while, I persuaded Frida to move with me to Masmiah, an old military camp located near Beer-Sheva. We moved there because we heard the accommodations were bigger and nicer than the ones we had in Bat Galim, where we'd lived as newlyweds. Meyer Berkovitch moved at the same time and we became partners. I worked in a garage as a mechanic and Meyer took my truck and delivered bread from the bakery, where I had found Frida a job, to the different farms in the area. After completing those deliveries in the early morning, I used my truck to deliver farm products into town, bringing merchandise to the stores. How similar my job was to the one my father performed just ten years prior when he delivered milk to people in Ungvar, but with a horse and carriage instead of a truck!

We lived in Masmiah for one year and were blessed with the birth of our first child, Ora, in 1953. We chose to give our children Israeli names to fit in with the then-current Israeli culture. Frida and I, however, spoke Yiddish at home, and we always called Ora "Perle," after my mother, despite the fact that in kindergarten, her teachers, friends, and cousins called her Ora.

Shortly after she was born, we moved to a *moshav*, a cooperative agricultural community of individual farms, called Kfar Achim, in southern Israel. The Jewish Agency (we knew it as *Sochnut*) provided for the *moshav* to give us a little farm with a house. We thought we would be able to pay for our farm over time. I continued to use my truck to deliver merchandise from the *moshav* to town.

Kfar Achim was divided into forty parcels of land (each with a ready-made home), and distributed one per family. Molvin and her husband also had a parcel in Kfar Achim, where they lived with their son, Yossi, who had been born in Czechoslovakia.

I was called for reserve duty in 1956, a requirement for all Israeli men after initial service, for what would be known as "the Suez War." I resumed my duties as transportation sergeant and stayed in the battle zone for months. I oversaw trucking transport and made sure that gas was delivered to tanks in the battlefield. We followed the tanks with jerry cans of gasoline.

Frida knitted me a beautiful sweater that I took with me, not only to keep warm, but also to have a constant reminder of our family close. While fulfilling my duty, I sat in a big truck, chock-full of jerry cans filled with gasoline. We heard airplanes above and saw we were being bombed. We jumped from the truck before it and the one next to us were hit. The gasoline exploded and the truck instantly became a pile of steel debris. But my sole concern was that I had lost my favorite sweater in that truck!

Another time I rode in one of the trucks with a driver and an army telephone operator in the back seat. We had an order to wait overnight because three to five high-ranking officers were going to head toward the Suez Canal in a jeep after dark. That night, our telephone operator got a call and gave me the order: wake up the crew in the trucks, get them ready, and drive into the desert to bring those high-ranking officers back. Specifically, I had to take the jeep with a driver and the telephone operator, who sat with his equipment in the back seat, and lead the rest of the transport. Our orders were to drive *exactly* twenty kilometers at *exactly* twenty kilometers per hour—no more and no less—and to watch the odometer carefully, making sure we went exactly that distance. Our ultimate destination was a mere eight kilometers (slightly less than five miles) from the Suez Canal.

While we drove the twenty kilometers, we knew there were Arabs hiding in the rocks along our path. These people wanted to kill us—

it was scary. When we had driven only nineteen kilometers, we saw someone running from the side of the road with his hands waving. We were sure it was an Arab and we were terrified. Instead, it turned out to be one of our high-ranking officers we were to pick up. We took him, and continued moving the transport, which included tanks. When we traveled the remaining kilometer, we stopped. I used my binoculars to look at the Suez Canal, only eight kilometers away. We waited there until morning light, at which time a helicopter flew over and ordered us to return to our starting point. I later learned that the United States had foiled our mission by ordering us to retreat, because no one was permitted closer than twenty-eight kilometers to the Suez Canal. In those days, we apparently took orders from the United States as well as our own government. We were quite angry.

I returned to the *moshav* after the war and continued working. Soon after establishing ourselves in Kfar Achim, I put together five or six business partners and we opened up a trucking company five kilometers away. These men had purchased additional trucks before we all went into business together, and we opened up a joint office. We named our company *Tachana Mercazit L'Tovalah*, the Transportation Depot. We connected ourselves to a bigger trucking company and obtained subcontracts from them.

I worked in this business, and Frida and I worked on our farm, for about eight years. My son Eli, short for Eliyahu and named for Frida's younger brother who died in the Holocaust, was born in 1958, during our time on the farm. We lived near Molvin and her husband and her two children, Yossi and Chava. It felt great to have a family again.

Chapter Thirteen

While Molvin and I lived on the farm, Arpie was in Canada and Helen was in the United States with her husband. Everyone I knew thought North America was the place to be! I routinely received letters from Arpie (who also shipped me a Frigidaire—we were the first in Kfar Achim to have one), which made me decide I wanted to move my family to Canada to be near him. Canada, however, would not grant me a visa. Arpie spoke with Helen and told her that I could get into the United States if she helped me. Helen sponsored me, but could not do so for the rest of my family. When I told others of my plan to go to the United States, people thought I would find money on the streets there. Although we were far from wealthy in Kfar Achim, because I had a Frigidaire and because I had the truck that I used to drive to Tel Aviv, my family was always viewed as being well off while we lived in Israel, just as we had been in Botfalva.

Frida and I discussed how we would move, since we had a five-year-old daughter and a baby son. We thought it would be foolish for the four of us to go without me having a job or knowing what I could or could not accomplish in America. Together, we decided it would be best for me to go alone and assess the job situation before the rest of the family came to join me. I left for America in February 1959, shortly after my thirtieth birthday.

I traveled by boat for fourteen days. Arpie, who owned a butcher shop in Canada, paid for my ticket. I arrived in New York, and Helen's ex-boyfriend, Itsu Polkovitch, also a friend from my younger days in Czechoslovakia and a Holocaust survivor, picked me up in a brand-new Oldsmobile. He lived in Philadelphia, but drove to New York to pick me up. Itsu worked with his uncle who had a bakery in Cherry Hill, New Jersey, and lived with his uncle on Bryn Mawr Avenue, in a Philadelphia suburb where I would later make my home. This day, however, he dropped me off at Helen and Willie's in Overbrook Park, Pennsylvania, a Philadelphia neighborhood with row homes, where I would stay awhile.

A day or two later, after I had settled in, Willie's friend Alex Leichtman took me job hunting. Soon thereafter, I found a job at an automobile garage on 51st and Walnut Street in Philadelphia. Since I had worked with or around trucks and cars for almost half of my life, it was a logical job for me. I worked ten hours a day, approximately five-and-a-half days a week. I earned thirty dollars a week. I spoke no English.

I did not pay room or board while I lived with Helen's family and was therefore able to save money. I missed my family desperately, though. Frida and I wrote letters back-and-forth to one another. Frida was scared, unsure of me and what I would do, since I was here with my sister with whom I had always been close. I felt badly that she was scared. I cried. And I am sure, halfway across the world, she did too.

I worked hard to be able to rent an apartment large enough for all four of us, and four or five months after arriving in America, I was able to rent a large, three-bedroom, corner apartment on the same block where I worked (51st and Walnut). It was a fifth-floor walk-up. With the money I saved, I bought a baby crib and two beds, some minimal furniture, and a hundred-dollar car—a ten or fifteen year-old Mercury. I was ready for my family to join me!

Excitedly, I wrote to Frida and told her to get ready to come because of the apartment, furniture, and car. I told her she should definitely bring our expensive Persian rug that we had in Israel, but otherwise, to sell everything else in order to purchase airplane tickets. I did not want Frida and my young children to endure a fourteen-day boat ride as I had.

Unfortunately, Frida was unable to sell my shares in the trucking company, so she relinquished them to the remaining partners in the corporation. She could barely afford our income taxes, so she sold whatever she needed to pay them and purchase the tickets to come.

When Frida stepped off the plane with Ora and Eli, she saw me and said, "I brought you your children." She only had their clothes. Nothing else. No money and, much to my chagrin, no rug! Obviously, what was most important to me was having my wife and children. Later, Frida told me that people in Kfar Achim told her not to carry the Persian rug overseas, because her husband was in America for five months and already had an apartment and a car—surely, he could afford to buy her a new Persian rug!

Chapter Fourteen

When Frida and the children arrived, I was still working at the garage. But, I needed tools. Helen went with me to Sears (my English was still not that good) and bought me thirty or forty dollars worth of tools and a toolbox. This was the equivalent of one month's rent for me, and was a very generous gift from Helen. She really helped me jump-start my career.

My boss gave me—and I took with pleasure—the dirtiest work at the garage. I slid under cars and stayed there for hours while I took out transmissions. An Israeli man used to stop at the garage to buy automatic transmissions. He and his partner owned a gas station on the busy intersection of Conshohocken State Road and City Line Avenue. One day, he spoke to me in Hebrew, so that my Italian boss could not understand, and asked me to come work for him at his gas station. He promised me better pay, and I said yes!

I worked at the new gas station for only a few days when my new boss asked me if I wanted to become a partner in the gas station. I told him that I did, but that I had no money to buy into the partnership. He offered to let me pay it off over time from my income, and that is exactly what happened. I became the partner in charge of the garage—my expertise—and he was in charge of the outside gas station, where all the gas pumps were.

It took me one year to pay off the partnership.

During this time, Frida found a job on 8th and Sansom Streets in an embroidery factory. Frida had always been excellent at knitting, sewing, and cooking. She took a night shift so that she could care for the children during the day. Frida was often alone in the big factory, to which she was given the keys. Essentially, I came home from work at night, we ate dinner together as a family, and then I drove Frida to work, with the kids in the car. Then, I took the kids home and put them to bed. At 5:00 AM, I left the children alone, asleep in the apartment, and picked Frida up.

Frida made some money while working at the factory, and I worked very hard at the station. Within a year or so, we saved enough for a down payment and actually bought a home of our own in 1960! At the time, we were under the impression we could buy a home for $800–900; I did not really understand the concept of a down payment and mortgage, but grasped that the monthly payment was not much more than the forty-dollar rent I had been paying all along! We bought a three-bedroom row house in the same neighborhood where Helen lived. I remember we had settled on it in the afternoon, and that evening, I sat on the steps of my new home: 1318 Westbury Drive. I could not believe that it was really mine. I had achieved the American dream.

Chapter Fifteen

Since 1960, my life has never been dull. A short time after paying off my partnership, I took over the entire gas station on City Line and Conshohocken and renamed it "Mike's Gulf." While I owned the gas station, Frida and I purchased and later sold other businesses, including diners, grocery stores, shoe stores, a taxicab company, an auto-parts shop, and, ultimately, an auto-repair shop. Frida ran most of our food-related businesses. She worked very long hours and doubled as a waitress and cashier when she was short-staffed. She contributed greatly to our household income so that we could give our children the very best we could afford. Frida and I became United States citizens together with our children. I remained at the gas station for approximately thirty-five years, at which time I sold it and devoted my time to other projects. My final project was creating an auto-repair shop that my son wanted to run. To this day, I still like to help out at the shop. I refuse to retire completely!

Frida and I attended graduations and weddings for our children, and later welcomed four grandchildren into our lives. We loved spending time with our family—it was a main priority. Frida enjoyed cooking family dinners and we loved having everyone together, especially on holidays.

In 1985, Frida and I accomplished another dream of ours—to own a single home. We purchased one in Bala Cynwyd, Pennsylvania, at 1301 Gainsboro Circle. We were so proud. We lived in that home for approximately fifteen years.

Around 1990, I started to realize I had a story to tell. I began sharing my experiences as a Holocaust survivor at elementary, middle, and high schools, colleges and universities, synagogues, Hebrew schools, and wherever else people would listen. Although I never had a formal English education, I soon realized, after getting reactions from people who would attend my presentations, that I was affecting people. With pride, I have kept almost each and every letter I received from a child, older student, organizational leader, or school after giving a presentation.

Epilogue

Frida and I returned to Botfalva in the 1980s, but we were able to do little more than drive by my childhood home, because our taxi driver refused to stop. A little less than two years after Frida passed away, in June 2008, I returned to Botfalva with my daughter, son-in-law, granddaughter, grandson-in-law, nephew, niece, and my niece's husband. The stark contrast between my life and the lives of my neighbors who remained in Botfalva highlighted the extraordinary journey on which my life took me. Being back in my old home, watching the cows come home at the same time, and tasting cherries from our cherry tree—still standing—made me think of my parents. I wish they could have lived to see what kind of man I had become, the family I raised, and the successes I accomplished.

My Family Today

Top row from left: My son Edward, his wife Jean, my grandson Avi (not pictured, his wife Abigail), my grandson-in-law Michael, my granddaughter Jennifer, my daughter Pearl, my son-in-law Jacky, my grandson-in-law Michael. Bottom row from left: My grandson Steven, my late wife Frida, me, my granddaughter Michelle (not pictured, my great-granddaughter Gabrielle)

Resource Appendix

Pletcher, Captain J.D., Berwyn, Illinois, of the 71st Infantry, the American liberators of Gunskirchen, *http://www.jewishvirtuallibrary.org/jsource/Holocaust/Gunskirchen.html*

Interesting Links

www1.yadvashem.org/odot_pdf/Microsoft%20word%20-%205880.pdf

http://www.jewishvirtuallibrary.org/jsource/Holocaust/Gunskirchen.html

Additional Photos

Me with Yudit, daughter of the couple who bought Zsiga's house from him in the 1950s.

The original wood-burning stove in Zsiga's house.

Delicious cherries from our tree.

(From left) My daughter Pearl, niece Chava, Yudit, Yudit's mother, me. (Below) My nephew Yossi.

Ilon, who was friendly with Helen but remembered the whole family, bringing out the newspaper clipping of the school photo to show us.

One of the original heaters from my home.

The latest owner of my childhood home, with me, and a bag of cherries Yudit gave me.

From left: My nephew Yossi, Avraham (my niece's husband), my niece Chava, my daughter Pearl, me, my granddaughter Jennifer, my son-in-law Jacky, and my grandson-in-law, Michael.

Our Cherry Tree Still Stands   69

A Sample of the Hundreds of Meaningful Letters from Those Who Have Heard Michael Herskovitz Speak

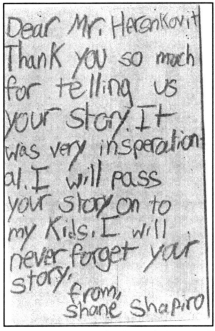

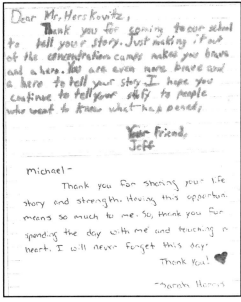

> Dear Mr. Herskovitz,
> Thank you for coming to Saint Anastasia school. It is such a privilege to have you explain your story of the Holocaust. I have realized that prejudice occurs across the world and we have to stop it so I will try my best to end prejudicey across the world.
>
> Thank you,
> Catherine Nguyen

> Dear Mr. Herskovitz,
> Thank you so much for taking the time to speak to us students about the Holocaust. Your story was extremely powerful and moving. I really enjoyed spending the time with you the unforgettable day. If you would like to contact me my email is ███ and my address is on the card. Once again, I appreciate you taking the time to speak about the Holocaust. I feel your story and others are important to tell so that our generation can pass them on.
>
> Sincerely,
> Eric Bisel

> Mr. Hershovitz,
> Thank you so much for sharing your life story with our school! You truly serve as an inspiration for all future generations.
>
> St. Anastasia School

Dear Mr. Herskovitz,
   Thank you so much for coming last week. I learned the real meaning about what people went through during the holocaust since I heard it from someone who went through it! I will make sure I pass down the story to my kids and hopefully the holocaust will never be forgotten. Thanks!

               Sincerely,
               Leila Gordon

Dear Mr. Herskovitz,
   Thank you so much for your kindness and warmth that you showed us.
   Your story is one we will never forget and meeting you a pleasure.
   We love Early One Saturday Morning and thank you for educating us about the Holocaust. Thank God you survived!
   You are a special man that touched our lives.

               Love,
               Paula and Kristin Frank
               Susan and Kayla Mannino

Jennifer K. Mittelman

> Dear Mr. Hershoritz,
> Thank you for speaking to us about the Holocaust. Now I know much more. I didn't fully understand what really happened in the concentration camps. You told me and now I know what a horrible thing happened. That will never happen again. You opened my eyes and now I and all the kids of my generation will try to make sure something like that will never happen again.
>
> From,
> Brendan Tate

> Dear Mr. HersKevitz,
> Thank you very much, Mr. HersKevitz, for coming to our school and talking about the Holocaust. It was very interesting. While you were talking I wrote down some of your information so I could use it in an essay contest about the Holocaust. I think it is a very interesting topic to read and learn about. It is a terrible thing and people who kill others for no reason what so ever, are terrible people. You are an extremely brave man for being able to talk about the bad things you have experienced. Please continue to help the world realize that such things should never happen again!
>
> Sincerely,
> Liz Cheefol

Dear Mr. Herskovitz,
    Thank you for comming to St. Anastasia School to talk to us about the Holocaust. Sometimes I have a hard time talking about the Holocaust because it is so sad. You have experienced the Holocaust and you still are able to talk about it. I will always remember you and your speech for the rest of my life. You have touched me and many others here at St. Annies. More than ten million people were in the Holocaust, you have went through a lot of tragic events but you survived. It amazes me how you are not mad at the Nazis. Thank You so much!!

    Good Wishes,
    Julia

Dear Mr. Herskovitz,
    Thankyou so much for your participation in Downingtown's Holocaust assembly. I can't find the words to express the way your story touched me. Even after reading <u>Night</u>, the horrific events became so much more real when listening to you speak. I find it inspiring that you have the courage to speak up, and I hope many others can take away from it as much as I did. Thanks again for your participation, and for sharing your unimaginable experiences with my generation.
    Sincerely,
    Mary Kate Interrante

SHIR AMI
Bucks County Jewish Congregation
101 Richboro Road, Newtown, PA 18940   (215) 968-3400

April 15, 1994

President
Delco-Stanton Lodge of B'rith Sholom
3939 Conshohocken Avenue
Philadelphia, PA 19131

Dear Sir,

Please accept this donation on behalf of the children of Shir Ami Religious School. We are making this donation in appreciation of Mr. Michael Herskovitz, who came and spoke to our young people about his harrowing experiences during the Holocaust.

The children and teachers were riveted to his account of the hardships he endured and impressed with his courage and willingness to share his story with them. We thank him very much and wish him health and strength for many years to come.

Shalom uv'racha,

Mark Elson

Cantor Mark Elson
Director of Education

ELLIOT M. STROM
Rabbi

ROBERT KATZENSTEIN
President

MARK ELSON
Cantor/Education Director

HILARY M. LEBOFF
Executive Director

BARBARA COHEN
Early Learning Center Director

The Delco Standard Newspaper

February is a month that a lot of great leaders were born. George Washington, Abe Lincoln, Charlie Marinelli, Lou Mason and Mike Herskovitz, to mention just a few. I like to write a few words on Mike Herskovitz who is a silent but forceful leader, a kind and just leader but also strong. Mike just celebrated his 65th birthday with his family and friends. He has health, family and friends who love him dearly. That makes him one of the wealthiest men on earth. Mike achieved all of this by hard work, because you have to work at life very hard in order to live it to its fullest. Mike and his family are wonderful people to know because we can learn a lot from a man who endured great hardships both physically and spiritually and yet he put his bitterness behind him and made a good life for himself and his family. His bad memories and experiences he put into a booklet so that all who read it, remember it, and stop it from happening to anyone on this earth ever again. Mike asked the question, Why me? The answer is simple....Many are called but only a few are chosen....Only those who can do the job. And Mike Herskovitz, you are doing a great job. God bless you and your family.

Fraternally,
Charles V. Marinelli, Jr.

May 5, 1995

Mr. M. Herskovitz
1301 Gainsboro Circle
Bala Cynwyd, Pa. 19004

Dear Mr. Herskovitz,
    Once again, I can't thank you enough for your time and efforts in educating our children. Even though we've done a great deal of research about the Holocaust, listening to someone tell first hand experiences leaves more of an impression on the children. They have been quoting things you told them in their research reports.
    The children were fascinated and horrified by your experiences. I have included some pictures of us for your collection and I I hope I you will be able to visit us again the next time I teach this unit. Thanks too for a copy of your book. I'm sorry I didn't ask you to sign it for me. Thanks again for everything.

Sincerely

Marilyn

Marilyn Shore
Houston School
Allens and Rural La.
Phila. Pa. 19119

2018 Kynwyd Road
Wilmington, DE 19810
May 17, 1995

Mr. Michael Herskovitz
1301 Gainsboro Circle
Bala Cynwyd, Pennsylvania 19004-2011

Dear Mr. Herskovitz:

I want to thank you for your presentation to the students at Congregation Ohev Shalom on April 26th. Although, unfortunately, I could not be there, I heard that our students were very moved by your presentation.

I am truly appreciative of the time that you put into sharing your story so that an understanding of our past can give our children strength for the future.

Many, many thanks, as well, for the copy of your book, Early One Saturday Morning. I was extremely moved by your story of survival and personal strength.

Very truly yours,

Eleanor Weinglass
Educational Director

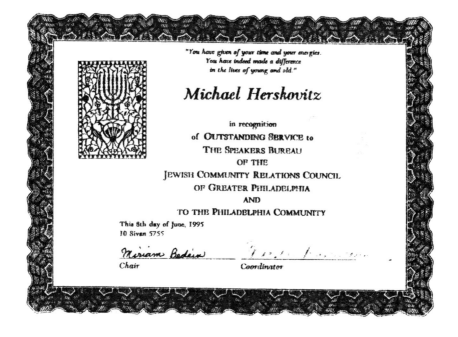

"You have given of your time and your energies. You have indeed made a difference in the lives of young and old."

Michael Herskovitz

in recognition

of OUTSTANDING SERVICE to

THE SPEAKERS BUREAU

OF THE

JEWISH COMMUNITY RELATIONS COUNCIL

OF GREATER PHILADELPHIA

AND

TO THE PHILADELPHIA COMMUNITY

This 8th day of June, 1995
10 Sivan 5755

Miriam Badain
Chair

Coordinator

CONGREGATION BETH EL - NER TAMID

RELIGIOUS SCHOOL
715 Paxon Hollow Road
Broomall, PA 19008

School Office
356-8028

Mr. Michael Herskovitz
1301 Gainsboro Circle
Bala Cynwyd, PA 19004

Dear Mr. Herskovitz,

On behalf of the children in the religious school I would like to thank you for sharing your very personal and meaningful life story with us.

The attentiveness of the students showed just how interested they were in what you had to say. Several of the students' parents have mentioned to me that their children were very touched by your presentation.

You are doing a great mitzvah and I wanted to thank you. In appreciation for your time and the copy of your memoirs which you kindly presented to us (and which I am looking forward to reading), a tree in Israel has been planted in your honor. You should recieve a certificate from JNF in several weeks.

Thanks again and Shalom,

Amy Blum
Principal

BETH AM ISRAEL

1301 Hagys Ford Road, Penn Valley, PA 19072 • Telephone: (610) 667-1651, Fax: 667-1652, Email: BAisrael@aol.com

Michael Herskovitz
1301 Gainsboro Circle
Bala Cynwyd, PA 19004

10 Iyar 5756
29 April 1996

Dear Michael,

Thanks again so much for your wonderful talk at the Yom Hashoah program. As usual, your presentation was very powerful, and was just the right conclusion to what I thought I was a very special evening for our whole community. Thanks for giving of yourself so generously, and for putting so much care and effort into your presentation.

I hope to see you and Frida again soon. (Please let me know the best way to return your videotape.)

B'shalom,

Rabbi Marc Margolius

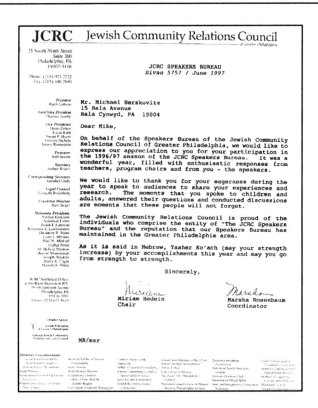

Jewish Community Relations Council
JCRC Of Greater Philadelphia

6 South 16th Street, 17th Floor, Philadelphia, PA 19102-3397 • (215) 922-7222 • Fax: (215) 440-7680
Email: info@jcrcphila.org

June 22, 1998 / 28 Sivan 5758

President
Ruth Laibson

First Vice President
Thomas Jacoby

Vice Presidents
Denis Cohen
Lazar Kleit
Susan P. Myers
Freema Nichols
James Rosenstein

Treasurer
Joel Beaver

Secretary
Arthur Krauss

Corresponding Secretary
Annabel Lindy

Legal Counsel
Kenneth Rosenberg

Executive Director
_ _t Siegel

...norary Presidents
Nathan Edelstein
Solomon Fisher
Judah I. Labovitz
Benjamin S. Loewenstein
Theodore R. Mann
Leon I. Mesirov
Paul N. Minkoff
Esther Polen
M. Melvin Shralow
Murray Shusterman
Joseph Smukler
Barry E. Ungar
Marion A. Wilen

JCRC Regional Office:
10100 Jamison Avenue
Philadelphia, PA
19116-3897
Phone: (215) 677-8810

Member Agency:
Jewish Federation of Greater Philadelphia
Jewish Council for Public Affairs

Michael Herskovitz
15 Bala Avenue
Bala Cynwyd, PA 19004

"Each day is a scroll, and you may write upon it what you wish."

Dear Mike,

You have chosen a day or evening to enhance the lives of others. You have brought your knowledge and your own special touch, together with 41 other JCRC speakers, to over 10,000 children and adults in the Greater Philadelphia area and have created a bond with these people that only you can do. These people will not forget the time that they spent with you nor your message.

We hope that your day or evening with the group to which you spoke enriched your life, too.

Your audiences have expressed their appreciation to you personally. We at the JCRC Speakers Bureau would also like to express our sincere gratitude to you for all you have done to bring information in such a responsible, objective manner to the public and to inspire people to discover and explore more about that the subject you addressed.

It is truly a privilege to work with each speaker on the JCRC Speakers Bureau.

Miriam Bedein
Chair

Norma Weiser
Vice Chair

Yasher ko'ach,

Marsha Rosenbaum
Coordinator

Marple Newtown Senior High School

Tolerance Day 2000 Symposium

In recognition of

Michael Herskowitz

as an historical natural resource for the teaching of the message of tolerance throughout the world. Our students have been forever changed by the sharing of your personal experiences in the Holocaust. For your dedication to the cause of tolerance, we thank you, and consider you a very special person and friend of Marple Newtown.

This 24th day of March in the year 2000

Donna Craig
Donna Craig, Tolerance Day 2000 Co-Chairperson

Keith Keyser
Keith Keyser, Tolerance Day 2000 Co-Chairperson

Marple Newtown Senior High School
Social Studies Department
**120 Media Line Road
Newtown Square, PA 19073**
(610)-359-4239

Monday, March 27, 2000

Mr. Michael Herskowitz
1301 Gainsboro Circle
Bala Cynwyd, PA 19004

Dear Michael:

    We are so grateful for your participation in our Tolerance Day 2000 Symposium here at Marple Newtown High School. It is our first endeavor at such an undertaking, and because of you, it has been a wonderful and extraordinary success. Evidence of this can be seen in the "Let it begin with me ..." statements enclosed. The students, faculty, support staff, and administrators have responded to your involvement in such an overwhelming and positive way, reinforcing our thinking that such an undertaking has been needed in our school for a long time. It goes without saying that we could not have done it without you.

    While we only were able to visit with you for a few hours during the day, we have come to know and love you in a real and personal way. You are so alive, friendly, and talkative (which is why we appreciate you so much), that we would like to consider you as a close friend.

    Your willingness to share your experiences, as traumatic as they were, speaks volumes about you and your dedication to the theme of our symposium, tolerance. We know that every time you speak, it is like reliving the events all over again, and it is for this reason that many choose not to speak in public about their own personal experiences. This makes you a very special person in our eyes and hearts. Without you, the message would fade into the dusty pages of history. It is something that we cannot forget, and must be reminded about every now and then. For, without remembrance, there stands the chance that something like the Holocaust might happen again.

    We applaud your efforts on our behalf, and extend our sincere desire that you will be able to continue to speak out about the need for tolerance in our world for many years to come. Once again, thank you for your participation in our symposium. Our thoughts will be with you as we remember the encouragement you have given us this day.

Yours truly,

Donna Craig
Donna Craig

Keith Keyser
Keith Keyser

TEMPLE  SHOLOM

ANDREA L. MEROW
RABBI

PINCHOS E. CHAZIN
RABBI EMERITUS

JACK BELITSKY
DIRECTOR OF EDUCATION

ARNOLD S. LURIE
PRESIDENT

VICE PRESIDENTS
MARSHALL COOPERMAN
SANDI GREENWALD
LEN KRAVITZ
SUSAN HANDIS

KATHEN KAUFMAN
TREASURER

NOGA GOLD
FINANCIAL SECRETARY

DAVID SHEINSON
ASSOCIATE TREASURER

PAST PRESIDENTS
ARTHUR L. ADAMS*
ABRAHAM ALBERT*
HARRY BLUMBERG*
ARLENE FILL
ISADORE ELEKOP*
MAURICE GOLD
JACOB E. GOLDBERG*
JACOB E. GOLDBERG*
DR. STANLEY GOODHART
LENNY HERRIN
HYMAN KORMAN*
SIDNEY PAWLOTSKY*
MARTIN STANLEY*
ISAAC RICHMAN*
DAVID SHEINSON
EDITH TOLL
MIKE ZALKIN
SAMUEL ZUCKERMAN*
DECEASED

23 April 2001
30 Nisan 5761

Mr. Michael Herskovitz
15 Bala Avenue
Bala Cynwyd, PA 19004

Dear Mr. Herskovitz:

A note of thanks for speaking to the students of the Temple Sholom Religious School. Your presentation was spellbinding – informative, emotional and extremely interesting. The children were involved in many questions and comments. I'm sure they came away from the morning knowing much more about the Holocaust and your experiences as a survivor.

Again, our appreciation for sharing your thoughts with us. May you continue to go from strength to strength in the great mitzvot you do.

Sincerely yours,

Jack Belitsky

Jack Belitsky
Director of Education

cc: Marsha Rosenbaum

Large Street & Roosevelt Boulevard, Philadelphia, Pennsylvania 19149 215.288.7600 FAX 215.288.7780

North Light Community Center
175 Green Lane • Philadelphia, Pennsylvania 19127
215-483-4800 • fax: 215-483-6728
www.northlightcommunitycenter.org
email: info@northlightcommunitycenter.org

Board of Directors
Ellen Berk Salom
President
Anthony Fischer
Vice President
Edward Dougherty
Secretary
Scott Simmons
Treasurer

Steven Blunt
George Dudzek
Janet Petkewicz
Gene Gilbert
Martina Griffin
Hope Heiser
Linda McBride
Christopher McGill
Stephen Obrimski
Dalia Owens
James P. Parrella, Jr.
L. Gerald Rigby
Thomas Scanlon
Walter Vogler
Cheryl L. Weiss
Linda Westphal

Irene A Madrak
Executive Director

June 18, 2003

Michael Herskovitz
29 Conshohocken State Road
Bala Cynwyd, PA 19004-3335

Dear Michael;

Thank you very much for the wonderful program you presented to the folks at North Light Community Center last Monday evening. I can't remember an occasion when so many people were so riveted to a speaker for so long a time.

I was especially happy for our young people because the whole concept of the World War and the death camps is completely foreign to them. They were absolutely engrossed in your story, which is almost unheard of for them. Our Youth Program director did a nice job of preparing them for it, but, even so, one cannot be 100% sure of the result. That success was truly in your commanding presentation.

I thank you for your patience with stragglers and want you to know that we are very grateful that you shared your remarkable experiences with us. It was an inspirational and unforgettable evening.

With all good wishes.

Sincerely,

Rosemary Twomey, CFRE
Director of Development

Please consider making a
contribution to United Way
and designating a part of
your gift to North Light
(#8001)

Partnering for a
Stronger Community

ARCHBISHOP RYAN HIGH SCHOOL
11201 ACADEMY ROAD   PHILADELPHIA, PA 19154
(215) 637-1800

October 18, 1998

Mr. Michael Herskovitz
Main Line Auto Center
15 Bala Avenue
Bala Cynwyd, PA 19004

Dear Mr. Herskovitz,

    I want to thank you on behalf of the students and faculty of Archbishop Ryan High School for your eloquent address to us on Wednesday October 7, 1998. Several teachers mentioned how deeply you affected them with the story of your traumatic childhood during the Holocaust. One teacher was visibly shaken with tears in her eyes as she related to me about her trip to Yad Vashem in Israel and how you had made the nightmare of the Holocaust so real for her. You put a young man's face upon a sometimes faceless horror.

    All the teachers present agreed that we want you to return to our school for another presentation in the Spring of 1999 around the time of the commemoration of Yom Ha'Shoah. You would then be able to address more students and teachers and tell them what was perpetrated against you and your family during World War II.

    But, I have to tell you, Mr. Herskovitz, what was most powerful about your life story. Although you and your family were treated in a most despicable manner you are not a bitter man. You showed the students that it is possible to forgive the worst offenses committed against you and to remain loving and caring toward others in your life. Yes, your story is a sad one. Yet, you left us with a deep sense of hope—hope for you, hope for us, and ultimately, hope for the human race. For all this, we thank you from the bottom of our hearts. We will keep you in our prayers.

Sincerely,

Carl A. Tori, Ph.D.
Chairman of Religious Studies
Archbishop Ryan High School

Downingtown High School West Campus

445 Manor Avenue • Downingtown, Pennsylvania 19335 • 610-269-4400 FAX 610-269-1801   *Home of the Whippets*

April 29, 2004

Dear Michael,

It is difficult to find the exact words or the exact phrases to express our gratitude and our appreciation for your willingness to be an honored guest at our fourth Holocaust Symposium. Throughout the year, we, as teachers, try to instill in our students the importance of education, tolerance, and acceptance of diversity.

Elie Wiesel reminds us that, "For the dead, and the living, we must bear witness." Please know that our students were touched by your presentation. Because of your presentation, our students can now put a face to events in history.

We are strengthened by your example, your fortitude and your compassion. Your words were heard and will be remembered- not for just one day, but for a lifetime.

The English Departments at Downingtown East and West High Schools extend our gratitude to you and we wish you good health and peace, until we meet again.

I will send you a copy of the photo we took of you and the video as soon as they are finished. I look forward to seeing you next spring. Thank you! Thank you! Thank you!

Nancy Robinson
English Department
Chairperson

Tony L. Watson	Patricia E. Bell	James L. Bruton	Paul E. Hurley, III	Ken Sigle
Principal	Assistant Principal	Assistant Principal	Assistant Principal	Athletic Director

April 30, 2006

Dear Mike,

    I would like to thank you for visiting Downingtown West. I enjoyed getting to know you throughout the day. This was an amazing experience and I learned so much from listening to you speak about your life. I feel much more educated about the Holocaust from your speech. I would like to thank you for giving me and my classmates the opportunity to learn more about what happened during the Holocaust. I hope you enjoyed your visit at my school. I also hope that you will return to Downingtown West next year to teach even more students. Thank you so much for sharing your personal stories. I really enjoyed listening to you speak and I really got something out of it. I hope you have a wonderful summer and return next year.

Sincerely,

Melissa Phillips
Melissa Phillips

April 30, 2006

Dear Mike,

    I would like to thank you for visiting Downingtown West. I enjoyed getting to know you throughout the day. This was an amazing experience and I learned so much from listening to you speak about your life. I feel much more educated about the Holocaust from your speech. I would like to thank you for giving me and my classmates the opportunity to learn more about what happened during the Holocaust. I hope you enjoyed your visit at my school. I also hope that you will return to Downingtown West next year to teach even more students. Thank you so much for sharing your personal stories. I really enjoyed listening to you speak and I really got something out of it. I hope you have a wonderful summer and return next year.

Sincerely,

Melissa Phillips
Melissa Phillips

Michael Herskovitz

From: "gilla robbins" <...>
To: "Michael Herskovitz" <...>
Sent: Sunday, April 29, 2007 12:38 AM
Subject: Re: April 27 2007 at 11:45 am

Mr. Herskovitz:

Thank you so very much for taking the time to speak to the 7th grade class at the Shipley School. The faculty and the kids were thrilled to have you and you brought to life much of the material that they had studied.

When I picked my daughter up on Friday afternoon one of her classmates came up to my car and thanked me for coordinating your visit, she said that she had learned so much from you and that she now had a better understanding of the stories and horror that she had read about.

It is a wonderful thing to give your time and make sure that history lives on. Thank you for providing that to me and the children.

Have a safe and wonderful trip and look forward to seeing you again one day soon.

shalom,

gilla

Lower Merion High School

Excellence in Education
Enter to learn, go forth to serve

David P. Piperato
Principal

June 12, 2007

Michael Herskovitz
20 Conshohocken State Road
Bala Cynwyd, PA 19004

Dear Mr. Herskovitz,

On behalf of the students and teachers from several History classes of Lower Merion High School, I would like to thank you for taking the time to come and to share with us your personal account of your life before, during, and after World War II. The experiences that you spoke about go well beyond what students can learn from a history book about this period. As we listened, we came to a greater appreciation of our own lives, particularly because the situations you described were so terrible for millions of people at this time. We admire your courage to make a life in America after the war was over.

We would also like to thank you very much for the donation of your book to our Lower Merion High School Library. Next school year we hope that you will accept our invitation to speak to other History classes. Your own attitudes and reflections about the past offer us a very positive message about the future. The Lower Merion community is very proud to have you as one of its members and for the many ways you demonstrate the fine character that resides here.

Sincerely,

Susan Naples
Susan Naples
Teacher of U. S. History

245 East Montgomery Avenue, Ardmore, PA 19003-3339

Downingtown High School West Campus
445 Manor Avenue • Downingtown, Pennsylvania 19335 • 610-269-4400 FAX 610-269-1801

Home of the Whippets

April 30, 2008

Dear Michael,

    Thank you once again for volunteering to speak at our eighth annual Holocaust Symposium. This program is so very special to us and we would not be able to bring something of this nature to our students without your help and support. This is the program that all of us look forward to each year; it continues to grow and received more and more community support. I know that our students are forever changed by your presence with us and by hearing your story. All members of our community are so touched every year by your willingness to share stories with us.

    We look forward to seeing you again next year. After so many years we truly feel as though you are a part of our families. Until then, stay well and know that you have a special place in the hearts of students, teachers and administrators at Downingtown High School East and West Campuses.

    I am enclosing a copy of the picture that we took on the day of your visit.

My heartfelt thank you,

Nancy

Nancy W. Robinson
English Department Chairperson

John R. Nodecker	Patricia E. Bell	James L. Bruton	Nicholas A. Indeglio	Ken Sigle
Principal	Assistant Principal	Assistant Principal	Assistant Principal	Athletic Director

> *"The reward for suffering is the experience,"* said Governor Rendell. *"Michael started by sharing the happiest, saddest, scary, and scariest moments of his life."* I was humbled in his presence.
>
> *Governor Edward Rendell   2007*
>
> **Moments in Time: You must have a Collage of Memories. Thank you for being here to tell the story. It can never happen again!**
> **Senator Barack Obama 2008**